Three Simple Questions

Three
Simple Questions

KNOWING THE GOD
OF LOVE, HOPE,
AND PURPOSE

Rueben P. Job

Abingdon Press
Nashville

THREE SIMPLE QUESTIONS

Library of Congress Cataloging-in-Publication Data

Job, Rueben P.
  Three simple questions / Rueben P. Job.
      p. cm.
  ISBN 978-1-4267-4154-8 (alk. paper)
  1. Christian life--Methodist authors. I. Title.
  BV4501.3.J6316 2011
  248.4'87--dc23

                                    2011031492.

        11 12 13 14 15 16 17 18 19 20—10 9 8 7 6 5 4 3 2 1

              Manufactured in Mexico

*With gratitude for all
who seek to live as Jesus lived*

Contents

Preface

Our identity is found and formed by the God we worship and serve. Our life together as Christians is discovered, held together, and lived out based on our understanding of the God we have come to know and seek to follow.

Reflecting on the three simple questions that follow can lead us to a new and fuller understanding about who God is, who we are as individuals, and who we are together as Christians and as God's human family.

We cannot escape the divisions, anger, hatred, and violence that are tearing apart the world that God so loved. Neither can we avoid the truth that so much of the anger, hatred, distrust, and division prevalent in the world has invaded the church.

In our honest moments, we know that this is not the way we want to live, should live, or are called to live by the God we have come to know through Jesus Christ. Thoughtful reflection brings the realization that the path we are on is not a path of fidelity or faithfulness to Jesus Christ. Rather, it is a path that leads us away from the very One we seek to follow. But what are we to do? It seems that the division, anger, hateful language, and even violence that are sweeping across the world have become contagious and the church has caught the disease.

Because I believe most of us do want to live a life of faithfulness and fidelity, I also believe that we are ready to once again get serious about our understanding of who God is, who we are, who we are together, and how we should live as creatures of the Creator God who has made all that is. Therefore, I invite you to a new exploration of these three simple questions with the confidence that they will lead you to a new understanding of the God of love who made you and a new understanding of yourself as a son or daughter of this God, as a part of the whole human family, and as a part of the living body of Christ in the world.

Who Is God?

———◊———

*Now Jesus himself was and is a joyous,
creative person. He does not allow us to
continue thinking of our Father who fills and
overflows space as a morose and miserable
monarch, a frustrated and petty parent, or a
policeman on prowl. One cannot think of God
in such ways while confronting Jesus'
declaration, "He that has seen me
has seen the Father."*
—Dallas Willard[1]

Who Is God?

*In the past, God spoke to our ancestors in many times
and many ways. But in these final days, he spoke to us
through a Son. God made his Son the heir of everything and created the world through him. The Son is
the light of God's glory and the imprint of God's being.
He maintains everything with his powerful message.*
(Hebrews 1:1-3a)

*"What you worship as unknown, I now proclaim to
you. God, who made the world and everything in it, is
Lord of heaven and earth. He doesn't live in temples
made with human hands. Nor is God served by
human hands, as though he needed something, since
he is the one who gives life, breath, and everything
else. From one person God created every human
nation to live on the whole earth, having determined
their appointed times and the boundaries of their
lands. . . . In fact, God isn't far away from any of us.
In God we live, move, and exist. As some of your own
poets said, 'We are his offspring.'"*
(Acts 17:23b-28)

She waited near where I was greeting people as
they left the service of worship, and when most had

left the sanctuary, she came up to me, shook my hand, and said, "Can you tell me more about God?" I soon discovered that her name was Anna and she was twelve years old. Her question was sincere; she really did want an answer.

I suggested we sit down and talk about her question while her parents waited for her in the area just outside the sanctuary. Racing through my mind were other questions. What had I said or failed to say in the sermon that prompted the question? What was missing in the liturgy, or present in the liturgy, that prompted the question? Had she raised the question in other places and at other times? What was her experience in confirmation class or Sunday school or in her home? One thing was clear: She was looking for guidance, direction, truth, light, and understanding, and she was looking to me to provide it.

In the brief time we had, I attempted to tell her of the God who is always beyond our ability to fully understand, who is greater in every way than anything we can imagine or comprehend, and who loves us always and in greater depth than we can describe. Since the One who created all things is always beyond us, we look to Jesus to see who God is and what this mighty and loving God is like.

Soon we moved toward where her parents were waiting, and I learned that they were supportive of their daughter's quest and grateful that her questions were taken seriously.

This conversation with Anna took place more than forty years ago, and it still informs and shapes my thinking and my living. *Who is God?* It is a question each one of us answers every day. Everyone reading these words, no matter your age or circumstance in life, follows someone or something. Each of us has our own image of God as personal and present, or absent and beyond us. Or we have some principle or practice that guides our thoughts and our actions.

We Name Our Gods

We may name God with our words, or we may choose to remain silent. But either way, each of us names our God by our actions—by how we choose to live. All of us live according to some principles we have adopted as our way of living. We may have thought carefully before making a decision about whom or what would guide our lives; or we may have pulled in behind someone else whose lifestyle, rhetoric, or reward system appealed to us or matched our hopes or prejudice; or we simply may have followed the path of least resistance and drifted to our present condition of following that path without question. But no one really escapes answering the question *Who is God?* Even agnostics and atheists follow some person, some value, some principle, some thing, or some overarching goal that determines the direction of their lives. They, as some of us who claim to believe in Jesus and the God he called *Abba*, may choose to remain silent. But their lives, like ours, betray the one who determines the direction of their lives. All of us give witness to the god or God who leads us and whom we follow.

You may remember the book *Your God Is Too Small*, by J. B. Phillips. As I look at my own ministry that began nearly sixty years ago, I am forced to admit that, far too often, I and the people I have led have been content with a god too small to be of any real consequence.

Far too often we are content with a god too small to be Creator of all that exists. We are content with our own form of a "tribal god" that belongs to us rather than a God who belongs to no one but who gives love, grace, and blessing to everyone.

Far too often we are content with a god too tame and domesticated to shake us to the very roots of our being and send us out of worship trembling in awe and amazement, clearly headed in a radical and countercultural direction.

Far too often we are content with a god who offers a band-aid for our wounded souls rather than the God of radical mercy, justice, and love—who forgives our sins and wipes them away just as soon as we offer that same forgiveness to those who may have wronged us; who not only forgives our sins but also heals our wounded souls, mends our broken relationships, and sends us on our way full of hope, confidence, trust, and strength to transform the world by living in the kingdom of God already being formed "on earth as it is in heaven."

Far too often we are content with proclaiming and following a god who is too unexciting to capture the minds and hearts of a world seeking healing for its deepest wounds, peace for its incessant wars, direction for its future, and companionship for its deep loneliness.

Far too often we are content to follow a god we can order around, insisting that our will be done and hiding from the truth of the gospel that teaches so clearly that what we pray for in the prayer Jesus taught is what we must practice in our daily lives. Unfortunately, "your kingdom come" is not a slogan or sound bite that has much appeal; so we choose to follow a god of our own making rather than the God revealed in the Scriptures, the Creation, and the life of Jesus.

Far too often we forget and need to be reminded by ancient and contemporary prophets that this loving God is a just God:

> The God of love is also the God of justice. The two are related, for in the Bible justice is the social form of love. Thus the God of love is not simply "nice" but has an edge, a passion for justice. God loves everybody and everything. . . . To take the God of love and justice seriously means to take justice seriously and to be aware that prolonged injustice has consequences."[2]

Far too often we do not hear the simple call of Jesus, "Follow me," and we become lost in following lesser gods. We know that consistently and faithfully teaching and living the gospel that Jesus taught and lived puts us in danger of being labeled too radical, too progressive, too peace-loving, too naïve, too much like Jesus. Unfortunately, our experience mirrors what has been a less than fully faithful pattern throughout the church.

Jesus Is the True Image of God

Despite our tendency sometimes to follow lesser gods, we know that, as Christians, the God we profess to follow is a particular God. We know that the call of Jesus to follow him is a call to follow the God he lovingly called *Abba* and to whom he fully gave his own life.

It is in Jesus that we have the clearest picture of who God is, what God does, and how God invites us to live as God's children. The writer of Colossians put it this way:

The Son is the image of the invisible God,
    the one who is first over all creation.
Because all things were created by him:
    both in the heavens and on the earth,
    the things that are visible and the things that
        are invisible. . . .
Because all the fullness of God was pleased to live
        in him,
    and he reconciled all things to himself through
        him—
    whether things on earth or in the heavens.
He brought peace through the blood of his
        cross. (1:15-16, 19-20)

This is the God revealed and made known to us through the Creation, the prophets, the events of history, the sacred word, the saints of God, and, most clearly, the life, ministry, death, and resurrection of Jesus Christ. In the life of Jesus we explicitly see this incomprehensible God who is not bound by our limitations or imprisoned in our preconceived ideas—a God who is greater than anything we can think, imagine, or fully comprehend.

The God Jesus reveals shatters all our little ideas about God and reveals a God who is author and creator of all there is. In Jesus we see a God who reverses the values of our culture and turns upside down our scheme of priorities, leaving us gasping at the sight of such bone-deep love, justice, and mercy. In Jesus we see such bold and radical truth that we tremble in awe and then cry out for help as we try to practice the faithful way of living he demonstrated so splendidly.

In Jesus we see a God who does the unexpected and the unpredictable. We see Jesus choosing to be the friend of sinners and being just as comfortable with the very wealthy as he is with the homeless beggar. We see a God who refuses to accept the boundaries that culture establishes and who moves with ease among scholars, religious leaders, soldiers, prostitutes, farmers, fishermen, tax collectors, and demon-possessed men and women—inviting them all into a new way of seeing the world, a new way of living, a new kingdom.

In Jesus we see a God who is not swayed by popular opinion, loud adulation, or noisy rebellion. In Jesus we see clearly a God who is not controlled by any ideology, philosophy, concept, force, or power.

In Jesus we see a God who is never under our control but always free of any control, and who may act and create as it seems wise and is in keeping with God's will.

Jesus reveals a God who is always and forever beyond us, completely other than we are, and yet who wants to come and dwell within us (John 14:23). Jesus reveals a God of love.

A God of Love

> *Everything that came from Jesus' lips worked like a magnifying glass to focus human awareness on the two most important facts about life: God's overwhelming love of humanity, and the need for people to accept that love and let it flow through them in the way water passes without obstruction through a sea anemone.*[3]

—Huston Smith

The Bible is filled with passages about a God who is best described and experienced as love. Psalm 25 and 1 John 4:7-12 declare this truth in powerful and memorable words and images that we can understand and relate to our own life experiences.

Who Is God?

Who of us does not need the forgiveness, steadfast love, and faithfulness of God?

> Be mindful of your mercy, O LORD, and of your
>   steadfast love,
>   for they have been from of old.
> Do not remember the sins of my youth or my
>   transgressions;
>   according to your steadfast love remember me,
>   for your goodness' sake, O LORD!
>   (Psalm 25:6-7 NRSV)

Who of us does not need to hear the comforting words of the prophet Hosea declaring God's tender love?

> I took them up in my arms;
>   but they did not know that I healed them.
> I led them with cords of human kindness,
>   with bands of love.
> I was to them like those
>   who lift infants to their cheeks.
> I bent down to them and fed them.
>   (Hosea 11:3b-4 NRSV)

And who does not need the frequent reminder that we are created in the image of God, and that God is love?

> Beloved, let us love one another, because love is from God; everyone who loves is born of God and knows God. Whoever does not love does not know God, for God is love. (1 John 4:7-8 NRSV)

Jesus reminds us that love is our connection to him and his beloved Abba. Our relationship to God and to each other is found, centered, and maintained by love:

> "As the Father loved me, I too have loved you. Remain in my love." (John 15:9)

The apostle Paul reminds us that we are to imitate this God of love in our own lives:

> Therefore, imitate God like dearly beloved children. Live your life with love, following the example of Christ, who loved us and gave himself for us. (Ephesians 5:1-2a)

It is clear from the experiences of the prophets and poets, Jesus, the apostles, and all the saints that have followed them—as well as from your experience and mine—that this way of love is neither easy nor strongly supported by our culture. It is a costly way, but also a deeply rewarding way. It is costly because we will find ourselves at odds with our culture and its practice of using violent words and acts to settle issues and to attempt to carve out "safety" assumed to be found in confrontation and violence. It is rewarding because there is the inner confirmation that it is the way of Jesus and the way for those who seek to follow him. And it is rewarding to experience the power of love in our lives to see the impact of the way of love in the lives of others.

Our culture, families, congregations, and everyone reading these words do not need more hatred and violence. Rather, we desperately need and deeply yearn for love and grace to heal our brokenness, mend our relationships, sustain us day by day, and light our path forward as we seek the way of peace and plenty for all of God's children.

Some have suggested that I speak and write too much about a God of love, and I confess that I try to hold ever before me the image of the God that Jesus followed, proclaimed, and knew as beloved Abba. It is this God who found me in the isolation of the North Dakota prairie; beckoned me to come near; and then offered redemption, companionship, guidance, opportunity, grace, and strength beyond my capacity to describe or explain. For sixty-five years this dance of love has grown; and today my relationship with the God of love made known in Jesus continues to confound me, delight me, challenge me, urge me on, and embrace me in a growing level of peace in the midst of a turbulent world.

A God Revealed to All

It is this loving, steadfast, unshakable God who hovered over all creation and declared that it was very good (Genesis 1:31). This same God, revealed in Jesus, calls all to come home and intentionally dwell in God's presence. It is this God who chooses to move all that is toward justice, peace, harmony, and plenty—not just for a few, but for all. In Jesus we see a God who is moving all things toward the kingdom of righteousness, the kingdom of God. This is the God we see at work in creation and in the lives of the faithful. This is the God we desire, the God we long for, the God we want to follow in Jesus Christ.

Our Christian creeds all declare our belief in one God while pointing to numerous sources of self-revelation by this God. We Christians worship a God who is revealed in many ways. That constant presence and quiet inner voice can speak as clearly as any voice we hear. And the Creation itself is an enormous gift of revelation of who God is and how God acts.

> The heavens are telling the glory of God;
>   and the firmament proclaims his handiwork.
> Day to day pours forth speech,
>   and night to night declares knowledge.
> There is no speech, nor are there words;
>   their voice is not heard;
> yet their voice goes out through all the earth,
>   and their words to the end of the world.
>   (Psalm 19:1-4 NRSV)

Scripture continues this revelation of God, which is most clearly and completely given in the life, death, and resurrection of Jesus Christ. Today that revelation is sustained and continued through the power and presence of God's Holy Spirit.

> "The Companion, the Holy Spirit, whom the Father will send in my name, will teach you everything and will remind you of everything I told you." (John 14:26)

So, we confidently trust the revelation we have of this one and mighty God and open ourselves for the continuing unfolding of truth as we choose to walk in companionship with the One who gives us life, promises never to leave us alone, and remains the One to whom we belong.

This God made known in so many ways has chosen to be revealed to each of us in ways that we may best understand. Is it any wonder, then, that we have different concepts of God and how God is known, followed, worshiped, honored, encountered, and companioned? In her book *A History of God*, Karen Armstrong reminds her readers that the rabbis taught that God could not be described by a formula as though God came to everyone in the same way.

While we joyfully follow and bear witness to God made known in Jesus, we also must remember that Jesus was born, lived, and died a devout Jew. This reminds us that the God we have come to know in Jesus Christ cannot be fully contained in any creedal statement, no matter how carefully constructed. God is always beyond our limited capacity to understand or experience. While we proclaim faithfully and boldly our own experience of and trust in God, we do so with humility and gentleness as we learn to live in a community of earnest God-seekers who may have experienced and come to know God in ways different than our own.

In his book *The Creed: What Christians Believe and Why It Matters,* Luke Timothy Johnson affirms: "The creeds' most radical and important confession comes right at the beginning: 'We believe in one God.' It is the root out of which all the rest grows. Without it nothing more can be said. . . . All language about God reaches into a mystery it cannot grasp or comprehend. Yet we need all the language we can get, since we recognize that, in the end, all language falls short."[4] There is great diversity in the practice of our Christian faith today as more and more cling to the concept of spiritual life and move away from creedal positions determined by others. This is not to say that we should forsake the hard work of serious theological reflection; rather, we should approach our neighbors' faith practices with humility, not arrogance. This requires the capacity to listen to another and to trust in the God who loves us both. God does speak in many ways, and wisdom suggests that we listen carefully before we make uninformed judgments about the revelation of God that others have received.

Every now and then we see splendid examples of what it means to follow God as made known in Jesus. These persons, both young and old, live out the gospel in such clear ways that their lives can be explained only by God's dwelling within them. "How like Jesus! How like God!" we may exclaim as we observe their lives of compassion, love, and grace. As we see them living as Jesus taught us to live, in our hearts we whisper, "I want to be like that; I want to live like that; I want to belong to God like that." And we can love like that; we can live like that. And living with these three simple questions can provide a sharp turn in that direction.

A Simple Practice

There was a time when most people could see a starry sky, a beautiful sunrise, and the bursting creativity of God in all of nature. But with massive population growth, migration to the cities of the world, and artificial light that blinds us to the wonder and mystery of creation, we look for other places to see God's handiwork unfold.

Today as you see the face of another, a bit of the sky, or a flourishing plant, remember the Creator God who upholds all that is and give thanks for daily evidence of that presence in our distracted world.

A Prayer

Creator God, author of all that is and lover of all that you have made, deepen our awareness of your mighty acts past and present and your constant presence with us every moment of our existence. Invade our minds, senses, and hearts like a quiet sunrise, a refreshing rain, a beautiful bouquet, a commanding voice, a trusted companion, and a loving touch—because we want to know you and remember who you are with every breath we take.

By the power of your grace, transform us more and more until we become beautiful reflections of your presence and likeness in all that we do and are, as we offer all that we are and have to you in the name and spirit of Christ. Amen.

Who Am I?

———————※———————

Remind yourself often,
"I am pure capacity for God."
—Macrina Wiederkehr[1]

"Who is my mother? Who are my brothers?"
He stretched out his hand toward his disciples and
said, "Look, here are my mother and my brothers.
Whoever does the will of my Father who is in
heaven is my brother, sister, and mother."
(Matthew 12:48-50)

Who Am I?

Dear friends, now we are God's children,
and it hasn't yet appeared what we will be.
(1 John 3:2)

While leading a weekend event for a congregation in one of our Midwestern states, the pastor invited me to visit the two nursing homes in the county seat town where he was fulfilling his ministry. As we went from room to room, I noticed that he touched the head or held the hand of every person we visited; and with his touch came some word of blessing, acceptance, and love. Then he said a brief prayer and we moved on to the next room. Occasionally, he asked me to speak a prayer or to read a verse of Scripture. But residents all wanted to see him, hear his words, and feel his touch. Near the end of the afternoon we entered a ward where nearly a dozen persons were seated in wheelchairs in a large circle. The pastor greeted the group and then again went from one to the next, offering a blessing, a word of love, and a touch. He went to people with outstretched arms and those with heads down, unable or unwilling to look up. He knelt beside their chairs and continued his ministry of offering a blessing, a word of love, and a gentle touch. I felt I was in a very sacred place saturated with divine presence because a pastor, perhaps unaware that his life was overflowing with divine presence, embraced every person he saw as a beloved child of God.

Sometimes in the confusion, tension, and hurry of life we forget who we really are. If we are to live whole, healthy, productive, and faithful lives, *Who am I?* is another profound question that invites our inquiry and satisfactory answer.

Most of us will not face the darkness that enveloped Dietrich Bonhoeffer, but most of us can identify with his confusion about his identity. We know what it means to waiver from brave and truthful disciples to frightened and timid witnesses. We also know, as did he, that ultimately and always we belong to God, and no power on earth or in heaven can snatch us from the security, identity, and safety of that belonging.

Who Am I?

Who am I? They often tell me
I would step from my cell's confinement
calmly, cheerfully, firmly,
like a squire from his country-house.

Who am I? They often tell me
I would talk to my warders
freely and friendly and clearly,
as though it were mine to command.

Who am I? They also tell me
I would bear the days of misfortune
equably, smilingly, proudly,
like one accustomed to win.

Am I then really all that which other men tell of?
Or am I only what I myself know of myself?
restless and longing and sick, like a bird in a cage,
struggling for breath, as though hands were
    compressing my throat,
yearning for colors, for flowers, for the voices of
    birds,
thirsting for words of kindness, for neighborliness,
trembling with anger at despotisms and petty
    humiliation,

tossing in expectation of great events,
powerlessly trembling for friends at an infinite
distance,
weary and empty at praying, at thinking, at
making,
faint, and ready to say farewell to it all?

Who am I? This or the other?
Am I one person today, and tomorrow another?
Am I both at once? A hypocrite before others,
and before myself a contemptibly woebegone
weakling?
Or is something within me still like a beaten
army,
fleeing in disorder from victory already achieved?

Who am I? They mock me, these lonely questions
of mine.
Whoever I am, thou knowest, O God, I am
thine!

—Dietrich Bonhoeffer[2]

A World in Darkness

Ours was a dark and frightening world when God sent light and life through the birth of a child. The Gospel of John puts it this way:

> In the beginning was the Word
>> and the Word was with God
>> and the Word was God. . . .
> What came into being
> through the Word was life,
>> and the life was the light for all people.
> The light shines in the darkness,
>> and the darkness doesn't extinguish the light.
>> (1:1, 3b-5)

God sent Jesus, the Word, into our dark world to bring life, light, hope, healing, and peace. Yet today much of the world still lies in darkness. Of course, there is unprecedented wealth and pleasure for a few; but multitudes of God's children live in the darkness of disease, disaster, hunger, poverty, oppression, and violence. The vast majority of our sisters and brothers struggle every day just to survive.

Far too often we witness national and global tragedies that result in the death and wounding of many. We also have seen political leaders divide communities, states, and nations by their rhetoric and actions. It is not a time to offer excuses or to place blame. But it is time for all Christians to remember who we are and to chart and follow a new path— a path that always moves away from violence and toward peace, a path that leads us away from the implied and symbolic threat of much of our national discourse, a path that affirms finding a way forward that benefits all and not just a few, a path that is in harmony with the One we claim as Lord and Savior, Jesus Christ, a path that I believe we all want to follow.

In this world darkened by confusion, deception, and dysfunction, it is easy to forget who we are. Even in our affluent nation, the tension, hurry, competitiveness, and false idols that surround us bring enormous stress to our identity as individuals. We struggle to remember who we are, and in our age of instant and constant communication, it becomes easy to attach labels to each other—and so difficult to put them away. It is often hard for us to see beyond a label and discover the beloved child of God who has been hidden by another's unfortunate choice of words or actions.

Those with a different theological position, lifestyle, or worldview than our own are often labeled as less than a child of God. Once in the "box" of someone else's label, it is impossible to get out because the one assigning the label has the key. Only when there is a retraction of the label can freedom come to the person placed in the box. The labels may be as general as one's ethnicity, biblical interpretation, sexual orientation, perceived theological position, national origin, education, wealth, or status. Or they can be as precise as one's style of worship, way of confessing faith, understanding of salvation, experience of being in relationship with God, or particular ways of living as a faithful follower of Jesus the Christ. The form that labeling takes is almost insignificant, for all forms of labeling are hurtful and are hard to overcome.

We Are the Beloved Children of God

In John 14:23, Jesus reminds us that we are invited to become a holy chalice in which God chooses to dwell: "Whoever loves me will keep my word. My Father will love them, and we will come to them and make our home with them." Even before we are fully aware of this truth, we are already claimed as children of God. We were made in God's image, and God chooses to dwell within us.

When each of us claims our full inheritance as a child of God, we see clearly that we are given this wonderful world to tend and to share as God's family. In the eyes of Jesus, we are not given a special place because of our birth, place of origin, wealth, gender, or occupation. As children of God, all receive an identity and place as God's beloved child. And those who choose to serve receive honorable mention. "Jesus called them over and said, 'You know that those who rule the Gentiles show off their authority over them and their high-ranking officials order them around. But that's not the way it will be with you. Whoever wants to be great among you will be your servant'" (Matthew 20:25-26). Serving others is following the way of love, justice, and truth.

In one of the darker moments of our national life, Martin Luther King, Jr. led our nation to a new understanding of love, justice, and truth. In his last presidential address to the Southern Christian Leadership Conference, he once again made clear the futility of violence and the power of love:

> I am concerned about a better world. I'm concerned about justice. I'm concerned about brotherhood. I'm concerned about truth. And when one is concerned about these, he can never advocate violence.... Through violence you may murder a hater, but you can't murder hate. Darkness cannot put out darkness. Only light can do that. And I say to you, I have also decided to stick to love. For I know that love is ultimately the only answer to mankind's problems.... I'm not talking about emotional bosh.... I'm talking about a strong, demanding love.... I have decided to love.[3]

We have seen too much hate and too much violence in word and action. Deep in our hearts we know there is a better way, and deep in our hearts we want to follow that way always. We begin that way by remembering who God is and who we are as God's children.

With these truths deeply imbedded in our lives, we, too, can decide to walk the way of love, justice, reconciliation, and peace because we want to walk in companionship with the One who is love and who calls us to love God and neighbor.

There is wisdom in the ancient story of a wise mentor who asked his students if they could tell when darkness was leaving and the light was coming. They gave many answers and finally gave up seeking the answer their mentor was helping them discover. The wise mentor then responded, "We know the darkness is leaving and the dawn is coming when we can see another person and know that this is our brother or our sister; otherwise, no matter what time it is, it is still dark."[4]

We are children of the light, children of God; and when we claim our full inheritance as children of God, we are able to see clearly and to know in the depth of our being that when we look at another human being, we are looking at a sister or brother who is God's beloved child, just as we are. When this happens, we see ourselves as we are and then are able to see others as they are.

Remembering Who We Are Through Prayer

There are many practices that establish who we are and remind us who we are as God's beloved children. Whenever we share God's grace, mercy, compassion, forgiveness, and love, we act as children of God. And in doing so, we confirm our identity as children of God. Our identity is not something we create but something that is given by the God who made us, leads us, sustains us, and loves us. We discover more of the full meaning of our identity as we seek a growing relationship with God through our acts of prayer and worship.

Walter Brueggemann said this about the practice of prayer:

> Prayer . . . is for the reception of identity one more time so that we do not forget who we are and who we are called to be. It is for sons and daughters returning one more time to the parent to receive our birthright. And in prayer we have to do with this parent who says, "you are my daughter," "you are my son." And then we are empowered to

decide what that identity and relationship mean and how we shall live out our lives. . . . Such practice of prayer leaves us authored, because we have to do with the One who is our author. We rise to live authorized lives, knowing who we are.[5]

We rise from prayer transformed because we have been intimately involved with the One who not only gives us life but also transforms our lives while leading us further and further into that grand design that God has for each of us. Prayer helps us know who we are and where we find the nurture, comfort, guidance, courage, and strength to live as children of God— bringing love, justice, peace, and reward. The reward is knowing who we are and claiming our inheritance as children of God—an inheritance that no one can take from us and that we cannot take from another.

We can, however, give up our own identity and inheritance. When we forget who we are and begin to see others as anything less than beloved children of God, we are giving up our identity and our inheritance as children of God. We are no longer following Jesus when we refuse to walk as he walked and refuse to obey

his command to love. But when we rise from prayer
confident of who we are as children of God, we are
equipped with the vision to see others as they are and
given the capacity to live as God's beloved children.
What a marvelous way to live.

A Simple Practice

Whenever he was troubled or dismayed, the reformer Martin Luther would remember his baptism. Roland Bainton writes, "Luther attached great importance to his baptism. When the Devil assailed him, he would answer, "I am baptized."[6] Remembering his baptism reassured Luther that he was a beloved child of God, that no threat could frighten him, and that no power could snatch him from the loving arms of God.

Those familiar with Luther's custom have found a practice of their own to remind themselves who they are, and it is something that can be practiced by all Christians. The practice is simply to speak your own name, put your fingers to your head, and repeat, "Remember who you are." As you do this, remember your baptism and affirm that you are a beloved child of God. Then offer a prayer of thanks. This simple practice can be a reassuring reminder of who we are as children of God.

A Prayer

Loving God,
Remind me often today where I find my identity.
May I never forget that I am your beloved child.
May I listen for and hear your faintest whisper,
Feel your slightest touch,
Respond quickly to your call,
Yield to your word of correction,
Rejoice in your companionship,
And serve you faithfully all the days of my life.

Thank you for hearing my prayers
And accepting my life.
I offer them to you as completely as I can
In the Name and Spirit of Jesus Christ. Amen.

Who Are We Together?

—————⟁—————

Saints are notoriously not interested in themselves,
but passionately interested in God and other souls.
—Evelyn Underhill[1]

The Lord is gracious and merciful,
slow to anger and abounding in steadfast love.
The Lord is good to all, and his compassion is
over all that he has made.
(Psalm 145:8-9 NRSV)

Who Are We Together?

You are all God's children through
faith in Christ Jesus.
(Galatians 3:26)

I encourage you to live as people worthy of
the call you received from God. Conduct yourselves
with all humility, gentleness, and patience.
Accept each other with love, and make an
effort to preserve the unity of the Spirit with the
peace that ties you together. You are one body and
one spirit just as God also called you in one hope.
(Ephesians 4:1b-4)

I grew up on a farm in central North Dakota, and
my earliest memories are of planting and harvesting
our crops with horse-drawn implements before we or
our neighbors had tractors. In the springtime I would
hurry home from school, do my assigned chores, and
hurry out to where my father was plowing with a two-
bottom plow pulled by five horses or seeding wheat,

oats, barley, or some other crop with a ten-foot-wide drill pulled by four horses.

No matter how cold, windy, or wet it was, I would walk behind the plow or stand on one of the little platforms of the drill until darkness came and my father decided to go home. Time and time again he would encourage me to go home and get warm. But no matter how tired, cold, or wet and miserable I was, I would not go home until darkness fell, my father unhitched the horses, and we went home together.

Why did I stay when the weather was beautiful and when it was absolutely miserable for a little boy? Because I would do almost anything and put up with almost any discomfort to be with the one who loved me.

The Way of Love

Living in community is not easy. Sometimes we are able to live together faithfully only when we remember that God is there with us, and that it is God's love that binds us together into the body of Christ.

As Christians, we worship and seek to follow the God of Abraham and Isaac; the God of Mary and Elizabeth; the God of Matthew, James, and John; the God of prophets and saints of every age; and the God made known most clearly in the life, death, and resurrection of Jesus Christ. In Jesus we have the best picture of who God is, how God acts in the world, and how God relates to us. In Jesus we discover the truth that you and I are God's beloved children, just like every other person on this good earth. We not only are "authored" by God; we are sustained by God every moment of our existence. Our destiny is to live in confidence and trust in loving relationship with this mighty God and with our neighbors—with all God's children—who are just like you and me. When we begin to live this way, we begin to love as God loves; we begin to love our neighbors as we love ourselves. This is the way of love. This is what it means to live in community.

When we reflect thoughtfully on community, we quickly recognize that there are significant barriers preventing community in this noisy, violent, divided, and dysfunctional world. As Tilden Edwards said, community is "what everybody wants, but almost no one is able to sustain well for long."[2] Asking ourselves the question *Who are we together?* can help us overcome these barriers and discover the essential elements to creating and sustaining a life together.

So, who are we together?

We Are a Human Family

First of all, we are members of the human race. Recent DNA studies confirm what biblical writers long understood: we are indeed one people. The scientific evidence is clear that we have shared DNA and points out that our ancestors came from the same part of the world. All people on the earth are *one family*.

Each of us is a member of this extended human family of God. God loves us as though each one of us was the only child of God in the world, just as God loves every other human being on the face of the earth. From Genesis to the Psalms and Prophets to the Gospels and Letters, the Bible reinforces this truth that Jesus taught and lived. To turn away from any of God's children is to turn away from God, who resides within, sustains, and loves each one beyond our comprehension, just as God loves us. Jesus said,

"The most important [commandment] is *Israel, listen! Our God is the one Lord, and you must love the Lord your God with all your heart, with all your being, with all your mind, and with all your strength.* The second is this, *You will love your neighbor as yourself.* No other commandment is greater than these." (Mark 12:29-31)

We Are a Faith Family

As Christians, we also are a faith family. In our contemporary world, however, it seems there is little agreement among Christians—as there is little agreement among all people—about who we are as God's children. We divide ourselves by race, social standing, wealth or income level, level of education, or what we consider right theology or pure living. There seems to have been an eclipse of what we Christians hold in common with all people as we use markers to distinguish ourselves or separate ourselves from the larger human family. Each division only makes it more difficult to remember who we are as God's beloved children.

It is a situation that makes us sad; and sometimes in the quiet moments of reflection and prayer, we hear ourselves asking the question the Twelve asked while they were at the table with Jesus on the night he was betrayed: "During the meal, Jesus said, 'I assure you that one of you will betray me—someone eating with me.' Deeply saddened, they asked him, one by one, 'It's not me, is it?'" (Mark 14:18-19).

Honesty requires us to invite God's Spirit to examine us and see where, how, and when we contribute to our brokenness as the body of Christ. What is it in us that makes it so difficult to see others as children of God who are loved by God and accepted by God as we believe we are loved and accepted by God? This was an issue for the Twelve and for the early followers of Jesus, just as it is an issue for us. There was the question of rank, privilege, position, and power in this new kingdom that Jesus described and lived.

But as the church listened to the Holy Spirit, they learned that the circle of the community that was being invited to follow Jesus was larger and more inclusive than anyone had imagined, and they were able to change and become an open and inviting community. As they did, they also became a thriving, compassionate mission movement that changed the world.

Peter's struggle with the Spirit on a rooftop in Joppa is a wonderful example of what happens when followers of Jesus are faithful and obedient to the instructions and power given by the Holy Spirit. Peter's encounter with the Spirit of God ended in ways he never could have imagined just hours earlier. One day later Peter gathered with a group that he thought he never would associate with and there proclaimed this revolutionary and nearly unbelievable message that changed the community of believers, changed the world, and now has changed us:

> "I really am learning that God doesn't show partiality to one group of people over another. Rather, in every nation, whoever worships him and does what is right is acceptable to him. This is the message of peace he sent to the Israelites by proclaiming the good news through Jesus Christ: He is Lord of all!" (Acts 10: 34-36)

It is hard to imagine what this moment was like for Peter and Cornelius and those gathered with them. Peter was clearly moving outside the rules when he agreed to meet with Gentiles. But he went because God intervened in his life and told him clearly that he should "never call a person impure or unclean" (Acts 10:28b). In obedience, Peter went where no one had gone before, taking wisdom and a vision that most of the world had never seen or heard. There must have been apprehension and fear among the people as the familiar ground of tradition and religion suddenly made a radical shift toward openness and inclusion at the direction of the Holy Spirit.

This message of inclusion is still a message we are learning today. Eugene Peterson, pastor, seminary professor, and prolific writer, reminds us that sometimes the church is far behind the Holy Spirit in discovering those whom Jesus invites into the Christian community:

> Soon or late those of us who follow Jesus find ourselves in the company of men and women who also want to get in on it. It doesn't take us long to

realize that many of these fellow volunteers and workers aren't much to our liking, and some of them we actively dislike—a mixed bag of saints and sinners, the saints sometimes harder to put up with than the sinners. Jesus doesn't seem to be very discriminating in the children he lets into his kitchen to help with the cooking.[3]

God doesn't show partiality to one group of people over another. Much to our surprise, God invites all to hear, receive, believe, and practice the good news. Philosophy professor and author Dallas Willard puts it this way:

Yet, in the gloom a light glimmers and glows. We have received an invitation. We are invited to make a pilgrimage—into the heart and life of God. The invitation has long been on public record. You can hardly look anywhere across the human scene and not encounter it. It is "blowing in the wind." A door of welcome seems open to everyone without exception. No person or circumstance other than our own decision can keep us away. "Whosoever will may come."[4]

Becoming Faithful Followers of Jesus

A good place to begin is to respond once again to the invitation of Jesus to "Come, follow me" (Matthew 4:19a) and to remind each other that we cannot become faithful followers of Jesus without the Spirit's help. Therefore, the only place to begin is with God. As long as we remain stuck in our own ways and closed to the Spirit of God, we will remain divided. But if we will review and renew our relationship with God through serious study and reflection on who God is, and if we will discover for ourselves the God revealed by and in Jesus, then we will be more likely to see others as God's children, remembering that God is Creator and we are always creatures of God's creative desire to form us in God's image.

No matter where we are in our prayer experience, we will begin to deepen our relationship with God as we deepen our practice of prayer and meditation upon Scripture. We cannot hope to follow God as revealed in Jesus if we never spend time together, allowing God to speak to us. On the other hand, the longer we intentionally live in God's presence—the longer we "hang out" with Jesus—the more like Jesus we become. The more we seek to remain in Christ's presence, the more the chalice of life that we have been given will be filled with divine presence, energy, wisdom, and direction.

But how do we remain in Christ's presence? Is our daily practice of our faith really about following Jesus, or is it about something else? Are we seeking his presence in the sacred places of life where he was found during his days on earth? When we remember that he was found not only in prayer and worship but also in service, where the wounds were, can we do any less?

Prophet and saint remind us that saying "Yes" to the invitation of Jesus to "Come, follow me" brings costs and rewards far beyond our wildest expectations. One of these rewards is the assurance, satisfaction, and pure delight of the awareness of living in Christ's presence as we follow where he leads. As we become companions of Christ, we naturally find ourselves at prayer, worship, and service, just as he practiced so consistently. The Gospel of Mark shows Jesus living these three streams of faithfulness so very well (see Mark 6:30-44).

The settings of prayer, worship, and service are the perfect environment for growth in understanding who God is, who we are as individuals, and who we are together.

How can we be companions of Christ today? By going where Jesus is already present and loving our neighbors as ourselves. It is easy to say, but it is not easy to do.

To say that I am a Christian is really quite simple, but to live as a faithful follower of Jesus is another matter. Taking seriously the message of Jesus can be frightening and foreboding, because in my honest moments I know that on my own I cannot live the way of love that Jesus taught and lived. When I look at the immediate consequences of his life, I realize that the way of love is asking too much, and I am simply not up to living that way.

And yet, sometimes when I am newly washed in grace and nearly overcome with God's love, I do get really brave and courageous. At times like that I declare my love and loyalty to God as revealed by the life of Jesus, and I think I am ready to live the life I so easily profess. Often sooner rather than later, I bump up against the reality of my life and of our world as I become aware of my self-interest that has overcome self-lessness and I realize the stain of greed on my heart and hands. Or perhaps I am faced with a loud and judgmental diatribe about one of God's beloved children. A brother or sister of mine is being ridiculed, demonized, lied about, and placed in the prison of another's judgment, and my courage evaporates. Far too often my response is silence. After all, I do not want to risk revealing my own weakness, or risk being trampled by a noisy and deceitful judgment. I do not want to be run over by the steamroller of propaganda or ideology that is loudly and effectively proclaimed as though it were truth. As my courage evaporates and my faith is exposed in its weakness, I realize that I cannot live on my own the faith I profess. This is asking too much of me!

Then, like a fresh burst of wind, the realization breaks in upon me: I am not asked to do this on my own! I am asked to follow Jesus, and that means not only to do and be what Jesus calls me to do and be, but also to accept the power and presence of God to make me more than I am and enable me to live as a beloved child of God.

Today the One who long ago said, "Come, follow me" also says, "Look, I myself will be with you every day until the end of this present age" (Matthew 28: 20b). When we remember the words and life of Jesus, following him becomes a matter of trust. Through the power of Christ in us, we lay aside all that is contrary to his life and teachings and take on all that exemplifies everything he taught and is today.

Trusting Christ can be difficult in times such as these. The loud thundering of the voices of division, partisanship, hatred, violence, and fear makes it difficult to hear the gentle voice of our tender Shepherd who seeks our attention. That is why we cultivate practices that help us hear not only the mighty rush of wind but also the gentle breeze of God's Holy Spirit sweeping over us at all times—practices such as placing ourselves in environments where God is clearly present and already at work. So, we gather with those who worship the one God we have come to know in Jesus Christ, offering ourselves as we receive the gifts of grace from prophetic word of correction to loving word of embrace; and we find our way to the wounded of the world, joining with those gathered to bind up their wounds.

As we do these things, we discover that we are living in an ever-deepening awareness of our companionship with Christ and that we are always suspended in God's presence, power, and love. In that presence we find an abundance of God's grace to sustain and keep us always. It is enough for this life and the life to come.

> My little children, I'm writing these things to you so that you don't sin. But if you do sin, we have an advocate with the Father, Jesus Christ the righteous one. He is God's way of dealing with our sins, not only ours but the sins of the whole world. This is how we know that we know him: if we keep his commandments. The one who claims, "I know him," while not keeping his commandments, is a liar, and the truth is not in this person. But the love of God is truly perfected in whoever keeps his word. This is how we know we are in him. The one who claims to remain in him ought to live in the same way as he lived. (1 John 2:1-6)

A Simple Practice

> Can a woman forget her nursing child,
>> or show no compassion for the child of her
>> womb?
> Even these may forget,
>> yet I will not forget you.
> See, I have inscribed you on the palms of my
>> hands. (Isaiah 49:15-16a NRSV)

Sit or stand quietly, fold your hands, and note how your fingers and hands embrace each other. Offer a prayer of thanksgiving for the God who embraces you in love and who has your name written on his hands.

A Prayer

Tender Shepherd,
Gather us together as your flock,
Defend us from division,
Save us from sin,
Lead us in paths of righteousness, justice, peace,
    unity, and love,
Help us to discern wisely and well your will and
    way,
And grant us grace to follow faithfully
Wherever you may lead us,
For we are yours
And want to follow you alone.
Grant us grace to do so, we pray,
In the Name and Spirit of Jesus Christ,
Who taught us to pray. . . .
"Our Father . . ."
Amen.

Epilogue

———✳———

"The end of all Christian belief and obedience,
witness and teaching, marriage and family, leisure
and work life, preaching and pastoral work is the
living of everything we know about God: life, life,
and more life. If we don't know where we are going,
any road will get us there. But if we have a
destination—in this case a life lived to the glory
of God—there is a well-marked way,
the Jesus-revealed Way."
—Eugene H. Peterson[1]

Epilogue

The one who claims to remain in [Christ]
ought to live in the same way as he lived.
(1 John 2:6)

Who Is God?
Who Am I?
Who Are We Together?

As we have reflected on these three simple questions,
we have discovered anew that

- God is greater than anything we can comprehend or imagine;
- each of us is God's beloved child, just like every
  other human being on God's good earth;

- all together we are God's family; and
- as Christians, we are the living body of Christ in the world.

Now that we are mindful of these things, how shall we live in this broken, wayward, and wounded world? Each of us is so small, weak, and easily distracted and disoriented by the power of the culture and the false gods that seek our allegiance, promising such stunning and shiny rewards that, when examined, are revealed to be empty—nothing but a sham or a scam. What, then, can we do?

We can remember who God is, who we are as individuals, and who we are together as part of God's entire human family.

We know we cannot do everything to change the world, but we can, by God's grace, each do our part. We can, each one of us, live what we are—a creature of the God who is Creator of all that is, a beloved child of God, a responsible member of God's global family, and a follower of Jesus Christ as a part of God's faithful family. Every day that we live as Jesus lived, we change the world.

A Guide for Daily Prayer

We live in a time of great uncertainty and stress. Yet it is a time of great promise, for the gospel promises that life can be good, peaceful, joyful, and splendid, even in times like these. The key to this kind of life in this kind of world is found in our relationship with God. Prayer is the link that keeps us connected to God in profound and intimate ways—ways that not only offer guidance, direction, and comfort, but also transform our lives and our way of living.

There are many ways to pray, and you, no doubt, have very likely established a healthy and robust life of prayer. If so, you yourself can expand the preceding paragraph to an entire book. If you have not, this is a wonderful time to begin the most important and fulfilling part of living a spiritual life.

What follows is a simple outline of prayer that you may use as a model and/or adapt for daily use. It is my hope and prayer that this simple outline of prayer will lead you into an ever deeper and more faithful relationship with God.

While the pattern for prayer is simple and easy to understand, a few words of explanation about each heading may be helpful. You begin with *Silence* as you prepare yourself for this intimate encounter with God. The silence will lead you to *Inviting God's Presence* into your life. Then you may wish to listen to God's Word through the *Scripture Reading* to see what God may be saying to you. Allow for *Personal Reflection and Response* to the *Scripture Reading*. This time of reflection and response will naturally lead you to *Prayer* and an *Offering of Self to God* as you are *Receiving God's Blessing* for your daily life.

You may need to adjust and modify this simple pattern of prayer to meet your own desires and needs, substituting your own Scriptures, readings, and personal prayers. My hope is that it will help you establish a deeper relationship with the One who loves you beyond our ability to comprehend and who has promised never to forsake you.

A Pattern for Daily Prayer

Silence
> Only in God do I find rest;
>> my salvation comes from him.
>
> Only God is my rock and my salvation—
>> my stronghold!—I won't be shaken anymore.
>> —Psalm 62:1-2

Inviting God's Presence
> Pursue the LORD and his strength;
>> seek his face always!
>
> Remember the wondrous works he has done,
>> all his marvelous work, and the justice he
>> declared.
>> —Psalm105:4-5

Scripture Reading
> Then he opened their minds to understand the
> scriptures.
>> —Luke 24:45

Personal Reflection and Response
> On the last and most important day of the festival,
> Jesus stood up and shouted,
>> "All who are thirsty should come to me!

All who believe in me should drink!
As the scriptures said concerning me,
Rivers of living water will flow out
    from within him."   —John 7:37-38

Prayer

"Have faith in God! . . . Therefore I say to you, whatever you pray and ask for, believe that you will receive it, and it will be so for you. And whenever you stand up to pray, if you have something against anyone, forgive so that your Father in heaven may forgive you your wrongdoings."

    —Mark 11:22b, 24-25

Offering of Self to God

Then I heard the Lord's voice saying, "Whom should I send, and who will go for us?" I said, "I'm here; send me." God said, "Go."   —Isaiah 6:8-9a

Receiving God's Blessing

Happy are those who trust in the LORD,
    who rely on the LORD.
They will be like trees planted by the streams,
    whose roots reach down to the water.
They won't be stressed in the time of drought
    or fail to bear fruit.   —Jeremiah 17:7-8

Notes and Acknowledgments

Who Is God?

1. *The Divine Conspiracy* (HarperOne, 1998), p. 64.
2. Marcus J. Borg, *The Heart of Christianity* (HarperSanFrancisco, 2003), p. 76.
3. *The Soul of Christianity* (HarperSanFrancisco, 2005), pp. 53-54.
4. *The Creed: What Christians Believe and Why It Matters* (Doubleday, 2003), pp. 65-66.

Who Am I?

1. *A Tree Full of Angels: Seeing the Holy in the Ordinary* (HarperOne, 1990), p. 27.
2. "Who Am I?" in Dietrich Bonhoeffer, *Letters and Papers from Prison,* The Enlarged Edition, SCM Press 1971 © SCM Press. Used by permission of Hymns Ancient & Modern Ltd.
   Reprinted with the permission of Scribner, a Division of Simon & Schuster, Inc. from LETTERS AND PAPERS FROM PRISON, REVISED, ENLARGED ED by Dietrich Bonhoeffer, translated from the German by R.H. Fuller, Frank Clark, et al. Copyright © 1953, 1967, 1971 by SCM Press Ltd. All rights reserved.
3. Martin Luther King, Jr., *A Testament of Hope: The Essential Writings of Martin Luther King, Jr.* Edited by James Melvin Washington (Harper & Row Publishers, San Francisco, 1986), pp. 249-250.
4. Richard Foster, *Prayer: Finding the Heart's True Home* (HarperOne, 1992), p. 249.

5. "Covenantal Spirituality," in *New Conversations* (The United Church of Christ, out of print), p. 8.
6. *Here I Stand: A Life of Martin Luther* (Abingdon Press, 1950), p. 367.

Who Are We Together?
1. *The Ways of the Spirit* (The Crossroad Publishing Company, 1993), p. 91.
2. *Living in the Presence* (HarperOne, 1995), p. 61.
3. *Christ Plays in Ten Thousand Places* (Eerdmans, 2005), p. 226.
4. *The Divine Conspiracy,* p. 11.

Epilogue
1. *Christ Plays in Ten Thousand Places,* p. 1.